Original title:
Aloe My Heart

Copyright © 2025 Creative Arts Management OÜ
All rights reserved.

Author: Maxwell Donovan
ISBN HARDBACK: 978-1-80581-867-0
ISBN PAPERBACK: 978-1-80581-394-1
ISBN EBOOK: 978-1-80581-867-0

Ferns and Feelings

In a forest of ferns, I dance with glee,
Each leaf whispers secrets, just between us three.
With every rustle, I giggle and twirl,
As nature spins tales, in this leafy whirl.

Oh, ferns are my friends, they're soft and spry,
They tickle my toes and make me sigh.
We share all our worries, beneath the sun,
In this clumsy ballet, where laughter's begun.

Textile of Thorns

Prickly companions, we've got a strange bond,
I wear my thorns proudly, just like a blonde.
They poke at my patience, but still, I adore,
These spiky little buddies who keep me in store.

With laughter and quips, we march through the day,
Creating a quilt stitched from humor and play.
Each jab a reminder, that life can be fun,
In this fabric of thorns, we're second to none.

Flourishing Emotions

In gardens of giggles, emotions sprout,
We water them daily, without a doubt.
With laughter as sunshine, they bloom and they grow,
Each chuckle and snicker, a delightful show.

From ticklish blooms to beaming bright rays,
We dance among petals in whimsical ways.
Together we flourish, oh, what a scene,
In this garden of feelings, we're silly and green.

The Blooming Heart

A heart full of humor, it blossoms with cheer,
It tickles my soul and makes worries disappear.
In a field of bright smiles, it's hard not to sway,
As joy wraps around me like vines in a play.

Each laugh is a petal, each joke is a bud,
Together they flourish, like flowers in mud.
From silly to sweet, let's dance and depart,
In this blooming delight, I cherish my heart.

Nature's Caress

In the garden, plants conspire,
Tickling toes, they never tire.
Leaves dance wildly in the breeze,
Whispering jokes among the trees.

Cacti giggle, prickles gleam,
Is that a plant or just a dream?
Violets chuckle in the sun,
Nature's pranks, oh what fun!

Healing Through Green

A leaf fell down, a funny sight,
I tripped and rolled, oh what a fright!
Yet up I stood, bruised not my pride,
For laughter blooms where greens abide.

Herbs whisper secrets, all around,
Tell me tales of joy abound.
Basil joking with the sage,
Nature's laughter, a happy page.

Verdant Emotions

The ferns confide in merry chats,
Discussing humans, chubby chaps.
Dandelions gleefully sway,
Belly laughing through the day.

Petals blush, their color bright,
When bees hum tunes, oh what a sight!
Flora's folly, spinning round,
A comedic show, where joy is found.

The Comfort of Leaves

Leaves, like hugs, from trees descend,
A cuddly comfort, my green friend.
Monkeying around, the ivy plays,
In leafy arms, we spend our days.

Sunlight peeks, a playful tease,
Kissing curls upon the leaves.
Even in chaos, calm they bring,
Nature's laughter, a gentle spring.

Love's Resilient Petals

In a garden wild and free,
Petals dance with glee,
They play hide and seek, oh so sweet,
In the sun, they find their beat.

When the rain falls down, they smile,
Sporting drip-drops with style,
Like a clown in bloom, what a sight,
Turning gray skies into delight.

They tickle the breeze, what a tease,
Filling air with laughter and ease,
Bouncing back from every fall,
These petals know to stand tall.

So next time you're feeling blue,
Just remember their chuckle too,
For in their laughter lies the key,
To love that's wild and carefree.

Soothe Me with Your Essence

A whiff of sweetness rides the air,
Just like a joke, it's hard to bear,
With each sniff, a grin appears,
Brightening up all of our years.

Your scent's a mix of joy and fun,
Like a prank that's never done,
In a world of chaos, be the balm,
With your laughter, everything's calm.

We sip from the mug of delight,
Your aroma's teasing, oh what a sight,
With every bubble in the brew,
I see your eyes, sparkling too.

So soothe me with your fragrant cheer,
Like a sunny day, my dear,
For in your essence, I find play,
Wrap me up, let's laugh away.

Succulent Secrets of Devotion

In the garden of love, we plant,
With secrets whispered, soft and chintz,
Each leaf a tale, each thorn a jest,
In this patch, we find our rest.

Updated vows in juicy bites,
Sharing laughter during nights,
Who knew devotion could be so spry?
Like a succulently hilarious pie.

Each secret's wrapped in green delight,
Waiting for you to hold it tight,
Blooming like a stand-up show,
In this romance, let humor flow.

So let us gather, cute and sly,
With laughter, we'll touch the sky,
For every leaf tells a bright story,
In this garden, let charm be our glory.

When Leaves Speak of Longing

When the breeze brings tales from the trees,
Leaves giggle like old friends with ease,
They whisper wishes, light and spry,
Spinning yarns under the twilight sky.

Each rustle carries a jest or two,
Expressing feelings, funny yet true,
Who knew longing had such flare?
Leaves have a knack for loving air.

In the dance of shadows, they tease and sway,
Reminding us to laugh through the fray,
When hearts pant for more than a glance,
The leaves invite us to join the dance.

So listen close to their playful call,
For in their chatter, love can enthrall,
With every wave upon the breeze,
Longing's just leaves having their cheese.

Nurtured by Nature's Graces

In a pot, you found your home,
With a smile, I watch you roam.
You bend and stretch, a silly sight,
Turning chores to pure delight.

Water spills, and I just laugh,
You soak it up, my green giraffe.
With sunlight bright, you dance and sway,
Prancing like it's holiday.

Neighbors peek and raise their eyes,
What's that plant, oh what a prize!
With your quirks, you steal the show,
A green companion, don't you know?

Life's a laugh with your leafy charm,
You keep me safe, you keep me warm.
In gardens full of love and cheer,
You're the friend who's always near.

Petals of Comfort and Care

Cracks in pots, a comic scene,
You thrive despite your quirky glean.
With a wiggle, you wave to me,
Oh how you love to be carefree!

Little bugs with tiny feet,
Come to join the green retreat.
With a giggle, I watch them play,
A garden party, hip hooray!

Each morning brings a sunny grin,
Your shadows dance, a grand win-win.
A sip of water, watch you glow,
Life's a festival, don't you know?

In the scent of leaves so sweet,
Every moment feels complete.
With petals soft, and laughter near,
You paint my world with joy, I cheer!

The Green Whisper of Togetherness

In a home that's full of cheer,
You're the laughter that I hold dear.
Each little leaf, a tale untold,
Our bond grows stronger, brave and bold.

With every snip, you kiss the air,
Fingers playful, without a care.
As we giggle and you sway,
Foundation grows in silliest way.

You share your breath, I feel your zest,
A friendship like ours, simply the best.
In every swirl of light and grace,
Together we make quite the place!

With puns and pranks, we rule this space,
In our world, there's endless space.
Every leaf a sly delight,
In our green haven, hearts take flight.

A Sanctuary of Sentiment

In this little leafy nook,
Stories blossom like a book.
You're the punchline in my day,
Together we laugh, come what may.

With sunny rays, we bask and play,
In our sanctuary, come what may.
You stretch and yawn, an emerald tease,
Each moment with you, a gentle breeze.

Oh, how we share these silly tales,
Where every day a new one pales.
With roots so deep, we both will grow,
In a dance of green, our love will show.

Near scents of soil, we both will thrive,
In this playful jungle, so alive.
A sanctuary bright, where laughter starts,
In this green embrace, join our hearts!

Evergreen Embrace

In the garden, I stand so proud,
With green friends all around.
Laughing leaves in gentle sway,
Sipping sunshine every day.

Prickly neighbors make me jump,
Yet they dress me in a clump.
Chasing bugs and birds on the run,
Oh what fun, just soaking sun!

With sharp-edged charms, they love to tease,
As breezes tickle through the trees.
We giggle as the bumblebees,
Join our dance with such unease.

So here we grow, a leafy gang,
Sharing joy when nature sang.
Amidst the blooms, we make a scene,
In our pot of mischief green!

Whispers in the Cradle of Nature

Amidst the leaves, secrets are said,
While other plants scratch their head.
Roses prattle, tulips snicker,
I humor them with my green sticker.

The daisies make such silly jokes,
About lazy, sun-baked folks.
We laugh and twist in playful glee,
Oh how lush our lives can be!

With sticks and stones, we build a throne,
Where petals laugh, and roots are shown.
Nature's whispers, soft and bright,
Inviting us to dance all night.

Together we make a raucous cheer,
Nature's melody, loud and clear.
In this cradle where we sway,
Every bloom finds joy each day!

The Pulse of Flora

In the heart of the green, a beat does thrum,
With flora friends, we're never glum.
Chortling ferns in breezy air,
We pop and giggle, without a care.

Saplings sprout with silly faces,
Joining in our leafy races.
Roots tap dance in soil warm,
Creating rhythms, wild and swarm.

Tiny insects join the play,
Buzzing tunes in a merry way.
Nature's pulse, a vibrant song,
In our world, where all belong.

So let us sway and twirl about,
In this garden, there's no doubt.
With each laugh, the flowers bloom,
We sing along to nature's tune!

Flourishing Under Sun-Kissed Skies

Beneath the sun, we stretch and sway,
Hoping that clouds will drift away.
With radiant grins, we wave goodbyes,
To gloomy thoughts that make us sighs.

Petals twinkle with a cheeky flair,
Spreading laughter through the air.
Botanical jokes in the breezes slide,
Joyful secrets we cannot hide.

Dancing roots beneath the soil,
Vibrant life in sunlit toil.
We share a giggle, a sunny wink,
Every day, our spirits link.

So here we thrive, with chuckles bound,
In harmony, our hearts are crowned.
Under sunlit skies, we bloom and play,
In this merry flora ballet!

Embrace of the Succulent

In a pot that's way too small,
A plant stands proud and tall.
I water it with all my might,
It drinks more than I do at night.

Spines that poke and have no kind,
Yet somehow, they ease my mind.
With leaves so green and full of cheer,
I whisper secrets with no fear.

Oh, how you thrive on neglect,
A plant with style and wit to reflect.
I envy your ability to chill,
While I rush, run, and pay my bills!

In your embrace, I find a laugh,
You crack me up, oh green staff.
A life so carefree, full of glee,
I wish I could be like thee!

Whispered Sentiments in Green

Oh little green friend, so fine,
You twist and curl, so divine.
I spill my woes, you soak them in,
With every leaf, I feel the win.

In your shade, I tell my jokes,
You giggle back, as laughter pokes.
You grow like weeds, while I just sit,
A master procrastinator I admit!

Friends call you odd—a cactus tease,
But to me, you're a live and squeaky breeze.
With spiky hugs, you keep it real,
Your humor brightens how I feel.

At parties, you'd steal the show,
All the chatter, you'd bestow.
Nature's humor, oh so sly,
With you around, how high I fly!

Nature's Tender Embrace

Wrapped in leaves, so snug and tight,
You're my cozy, green delight.
With every poke, a giggle springs,
You're the joy that nature brings.

Through sunny days and rainy moods,
You lift my spirits, oh, dear dude.
I chat with you, you nod along,
Our funny bond, it feels so strong.

Though others fear your prickly face,
I see the charm, a timeless grace.
A charmer in a plant pot's guise,
With every chat, I grow so wise.

In your company, I find my groove,
A succulent dance, we both approve.
With every quirk, you make me grin,
Nature's wisdom, where do I begin?

The Healing Touch of Flora

With every scratch and poke I feel,
Your healing touch is quite unreal.
A green companion in the fray,
You brighten up my wacky day.

As I bump into you in glee,
You tease and laugh, so carefree.
In a world of chaos, you stand still,
A stick of joy, a breath to thrill.

Though I may trip and fall on ground,
You bring me laughter all around.
A partner in my silly plight,
You spark a giggle, pure delight.

In the garden, we're quite a pair,
You wiggle there, always rare.
With every hug, a chuckle flows,
Your prickly love, oh how it grows!

Heartfelt Healing

In my garden, you reside,
With leaves so wide,
You soak up the sun,
And I can't help but run.

You're not just a plant,
But my cuddly friend,
With your spiky embrace,
Who needs to pretend?

Water you ask for, that's a treat,
I swear you're not here just to eat.
You're my buddy in this green spree,
Chillin' in the breeze, just you and me.

So laughter sprouts as we shake and sway,
You brighten my dullest of days.
Healing with humor might be a start,
Together we bloom, oh kindred heart.

The Lush Sanctuary

In a corner bright, you stand tall,
With your suave poses, you enthrall.
A playful giggle, a wink so sly,
Who knew plants could be such a spry?

You soak in attention, oh so keen,
In this lush retreat, we're quite the scene.
With dirt on my hands, I feel so grand,
Together we plot, like a leafy band.

Photosynthesis? Such a fancy word!
But really, you just wish to be heard.
Your silent whispers echo through,
Make me chuckle, oh how you do!

Between sun and shade, we laugh and play,
In this vibrant world, we bloom and sway.
Happiness crafted in nature's art,
You're my leafy joy, oh playful heart.

Quietude in Bloom

In the calm of the day, you're my muse,
With plucky little leaves, how can I lose?
Your stillness soaks up the laughter,
What joy you bring, happily ever after!

Though you seem quiet, you've got a role,
To tickle my funny bone, that's your goal.
With every sprout, my silliness grows,
Who knew a plant could cause such a prose?

In your shade, I daydream and smile,
Creating tales that stretch for a mile.
You nod along as I tell my story,
With you here, life's a bit more hoary!

So let's twirl in this gentle spell,
In this blooming silence, all is well.
With humor entwined in nature's art,
You're a quiet joy, oh cherished heart.

Rooted Affection

You sit so still but speak so loud,
With those pokey leaves, you make me proud.
In a quirky way, you're my best mate,
A plant with a cheerleading trait!

Filling my day with vibrant green,
Your humor shines bright, always seen.
When sunlight dances, you're in the mood,
Bouncing joyfully, my leafy dude!

You've got a talent for making me grin,
In this pot of life, where we both win.
Your wit's as sharp as a thorny surprise,
Just when I need it, hilarious skies!

So here's to the endless chuckles we share,
With roots intertwined, nothing can compare.
In this little world, you're pure delight,
With laughter and love, our spirits take flight.

Tender Greens and Hidden Yearnings

In a pot where dreams reside,
A plant with quirks, a leafy guide.
It sways to tunes from far away,
Telling secrets in a leafy ballet.

With every sip of morning dew,
It giggles softly, just like you.
Those tender greens hold laughter tight,
In hidden yearnings, sheer delight.

Its arms reach out, a playful show,
Waving gently to the garden below.
Whispers of joy in each new sprout,
A funny dance, no shadow of doubt.

So here we share our leafy spree,
In every twist, a touch of glee.
A heart so full, a pot so bright,
We bloom together, pure delight.

Blooming beneath the Stars

Beneath the stars, where dreams take flight,
A plant does pirouettes at night.
With every twinkle, it shares a grin,
In moonlit laughter, joys begin.

It sings to crickets, sways to the breeze,
With whimsy and fun, it aims to please.
Each petal whispers tales of cheer,
In the garden's laughter, we hold dear.

There's magic in its leafy style,
A giggle hidden in every aisle.
In the darkness, it makes a mess,
Yet brings the glow, a funny dress.

So come and dance, oh night so bright,
Let's sway together till morning light.
In blooming joy beneath the sky,
Our hearts entwine, a sweet reply.

In the Shade of Everlasting Care

In the shade where giggles grow,
A plant unravels life's odd flow.
With every breeze, it tells a tale,
Of silly moments, not for sale.

The sun tickles with a golden tease,
While shadows waltz with the gentle breeze.
Its leaves, they whisper, dance for fun,
In this garden, we've just begun.

When raindrops fall, they tap-dance too,
On every leaf, a playful crew.
And in that shade, with laughter bright,
We share our quirks 'til day turns night.

So pull up a chair and stay awhile,
Let's nurture joy with every smile.
In love's embrace, we'll linger there,
In the shade of endless care.

The Language of Growing Affection

In whispers soft, a tale unfolds,
In every sprout, a love that holds.
Through playful roots and leafy style,
A language formed, an endless smile.

Each morning brings a funny twist,
A dance of light that can't be missed.
The silliest blooms with colors bright,
All speak the truth of pure delight.

With every leaf, a giggle shared,
In this green world, we've been compared.
Through laughter's growth, we come alive,
In this affection, together we thrive.

So here's to us, to love's embrace,
In nature's laughter, we find our place.
With hearts so green, we laugh and play,
In the garden of joy, we'll forever stay.

Ethereal Hues and Heartfelt Melds

In a pot sitting snug on my sill,
The leaves twist and shout with a thrill.
Each morning I chat, a peculiar sight,
It nods back at me, full of delight.

With sunlight pouring, it dances a jig,
So paranoid, it hides in a fig.
I offer it water, a sip and a swig,
It's my loyal buddy, my little green twig.

When it's prickly with glee, I giggle away,
In this leafy affair, we both love to play.
Oh, the stories we share, bright as a spark,
In the warmth of our home, we brighten the dark.

Together we wander, around my abode,
Sprinkling joy, lightening the load.
These moments are silly, but I hold them near,
In my leafy companion, there's little fear.

The Poetry of Greenery

A slice of green, in my window it beams,
With quirky designs and sunlit dreams.
I swear it's plotting a grand escape,
With plans so wild, they take shape.

Each time I pass by, it gives me a grin,
Encouraging laughs, a mischievous twin.
We dream of gardens beyond that glass,
Where the sun shines brighter and worries don't last.

In a world full of chaos, it laughs with glee,
Reminding me life can be silly and free.
Together we twirl, a duet so sweet,
In the jazz of existence, we dance on our feet.

I toss it a chip, it's snack time for two,
But my little friend claims it's not quite true.
With each witty quirk, I chuckle and sway,
In the poetry of greenery, we find our way.

Growing Together in Nature's Glow

In our little corner, we bloom and we shine,
Two oddities twirling, sipping on thyme.
You can't take this humor, it's rooted so deep,
Like my silly plant, it's hard to keep.

Twisting and turning, it catches the breeze,
While I laugh 'til I cry, my whims it appease.
With petals like skirts and stems proud and tall,
In this dance of the strange, we relish it all.

When laughter erupts like sudden rain,
We revel in joy, shake off the mundane.
With jokes that sprout just like we do,
Who knew a plant could be such a hoot too?

Together we thrive, in unruly delight,
Nurturing giggles from morning to night.
In nature's embrace, we've found our sun,
An odd, funny duo, forever as one.

Cacti Dreams and Desert Whispers

In a land where spines can cuddle,
I found a plant that tells a muddle.
It whispers jokes, oh what a tease,
With every poke, it brings me ease.

Sun rays dance on prickly tops,
As laughter blooms, no need for props.
I hear it chuckle in the breeze,
A comedy of thorns and leaves.

The lizards laugh; they know the game,
In this wild world, we share the fame.
In cacti dreams, we play so bright,
A funny tale in desert light.

With every step, the sand does shift,
Nature's humor is the gift.
In piercing friendships, we all find,
A joy that's woven, intertwined.

Where Love Takes Root

In the garden where giggles grow,
Love plants seeds; we always sow.
With tangled vines and silly puns,
We share our jokes, we share our runs.

Petals blush while roots entwine,
Beneath the sun, our hearts align.
With every sprout, we rise and play,
In this silly dance, we sway.

A leafy hug, a playful poke,
Our laughter blooms beneath the oak.
Beneath the surface, joy does dwell,
In gardening love, all's well.

We water dreams with jests and cheer,
In this patch, there's nothing to fear.
So let our love grow wild and free,
In the roots of humor, just you and me.

Nature's Love Letters

In every leaf, a note I find,
The trees and blooms, so sweetly kind.
Their laughter whispers through the air,
Nature's notes, beyond compare.

The roses write with petal ink,
While dandelions pause to wink.
In this love letter, spice and fun,
A chorus sung by everyone.

The bee hums tunes of joy and light,
While butterflies take wing in flight.
Each day unfolds the silliest tales,
On nature's wind, our laughter sails.

Through roots and branches, stories flow,
A vibrant world where giggles grow.
Let's read the leaves, from here to there,
In nature's hearts, we find our share.

Roots That Bind Us

Beneath the soil, our roots unite,
Through jests and quirks, we find delight.
With tangled laughter, hearts unearth,
A bond of joy, a thriving girth.

The daisies crack their silly jokes,
While busy ants perform their hoax.
In this shared ground, we all belong,
Roots that bind us, forever strong.

With every twist, our stories blend,
In this vibrant patch, we never end.
We weave our tales with daily glee,
Nature's comedy, wild and free.

So let us dance in this warm embrace,
With nature's chuckles, life's sweet grace.
In every root, a truth runs deep,
In laughter's arms, our hearts will leap.

The Heart's Botanical Haven

In a garden filled with giggles bright,
Plants sway gently in the light.
They whisper jokes from stem to leaf,
Causing bursts of silly grief.

Cacti wear their prickles proud,
Dancing solo, never loud.
While daisies play hide and seek,
Tickling toes, they hide and peek.

Sunflowers boast in fields of cheer,
Telling tales of yesteryear.
With petals bright, they play the part,
A blooming laugh, a joy-filled art.

In this haven of green delight,
Every bloom brings smiles so bright.
So, come and laugh, don't be shy,
In this vibrant garden, let joy fly!

Petals of Quietude

In the stillness, petals dance,
With every sway, they take a chance.
Whispers float on warmest air,
A chuckle here, a knowing stare.

The tulips tease with colors bold,
Each a secret yet untold.
They giggle soft, their stories weave,
In quiet tones, they softly grieve.

Lavender laughs, a fragrant jest,
While sage just chuckles, doing its best.
They share their dreams, on breezy nights,
Turning moments into giggling flights.

Oh, petals soft, you know the score,
With every breeze, we crave for more.
In this quiet, we find our glee,
Nature's humor, wild and free!

Secrets of the Earth's Love

Roots entwined, a tangled plot,
Nature's love, a funny lot.
With dirt-streaked faces, plants conspire,
To make us laugh, their one desire.

The roses blush, a giggly tease,
"Watch out for thorns!" they say with ease.
Violets wink, with mischief sly,
Mocking clouds that drift on by.

Ferns unfurl with a sly grin,
"Join our dance, let laughter begin!"
In every leaf, a chuckle grows,
Nature's secrets, only we know.

With every bloom, the giggles swell,
In this garden where laughter dwells.
So keep your heart, and let it flutter,
With every whisper, let's bring the butter!

Flora's Promise to the Soul

In this realm where laughter springs,
Flowers promise delightful things.
A comedy of roots and leaves,
In every petal, joy perceives.

Forget-me-nots wink, "We're here to stay!"
While lilies laugh the day away.
In this patch of sunlit cheer,
Each bloom declares, "We're glad you're here!"

Chrysanthemum chuckles, bold and loud,
As pansies peek from behind a cloud.
Together, they share a leafy jest,
Making every heart feel truly blessed.

So come and dance amongst the green,
Where happy blooms can be seen.
In flora's arms, our spirits soar,
Laughter's magic forevermore!

Growth Stories from Every Leaf

In the garden, I plant with glee,
A little sprout just loves to tease.
It wiggles and giggles, what a sight,
Saying, "Water me or I'll take flight!"

With sunshine, it dances, sways with grace,
As I chase it all over the place.
Its leaves tell tales of woe and cheer,
In the wind, whispers I long to hear.

When the rain comes, it splashes around,
"I'm growing taller, don't you frown!"
Yet when I prune, it acts all coy,
"Oh dear, does it hurt? Or bring me joy?"

A buddy of mine, oh what a show,
It talks to me, you really should know.
With roots entwined, we share small laughs,
A quirky plant friend, my leafy halves.

Green Heartbeats of Affection

In the sunlight, oh, what a source,
My little plant, it shows decorum, of course.
With fronds that wave like a hand in the air,
I swear it's got charm, a real love affair!

As I nurture, it gives a cheeky grin,
With every drop, it knows it will win.
"Water me, darling, I'm so parched!"
It calls out loud, like a lively march!

Roots bonding strong, as partners in crime,
It steals my snacks—oh, how sublime!
Photosynthesis dance, such a hilarious plot,
Who knew a plant could be such a tot?

They say green thumbs bring tales of old,
But this little buddy breaks all molds.
With each heartbeat, leaves flutter and quirk,
We share our secrets, an odd little perk.

Emotions Seeded in Soil

In a pot so snug, emotions bloom,
A seed of laughter dispelling gloom.
It stretches out, seeking the skies,
With roots that tickle, oh what a surprise!

Composting dreams, it stirs the ground,
"Guess what, gardener? I'm feeling profound!"
I laugh and reply, "Just don't get too high,
I need you to stay, my leafy ally!"

Soil gets whispered confessions galore,
"Dig deep into feelings, there's always more!"
With every shovel of dirt is a chuckle,
As my plant shares its hopes, oh the snuggle!

So here we are, in a humorous dance,
Growing together, we take our chance.
Love sprinkled softly like dew on a morn,
With laughter and joy, new life is born.

Life's Nurtured Expressions

Little green fingers reach out to play,
With photosynthesis as the game they display.
Each leaf a grin, cheeky and bright,
Telling the sun, "I'm ready for light!"

In whimsical whispers, roots quietly chatter,
Sharing secrets of soil, oh, what's the matter?
"No need to fret!" they giggle and tease,
"In the dance of growth, we're aiming to please!"

As branches sway, it's a ripple of fun,
"Did you hear that? We're second to none!"
Through the seasons, we twirl and we leap,
In this garden of laughter, nothing's too deep!

Life's little expressions sprout with a grin,
For nothing can stop this joy from within.
With every green leaf, a chuckle we leave,
Growing together, what treasures we weave!

Embracing Nature's Love Story

In a pot, she sits so spry,
Green goddess with a winked eye.
Her leaves dance in the sunshine,
Whispering secrets of the divine.

She teases the cactus with her flair,
Says, "Join me, if you dare!"
While the daisies snicker and bloom,
We laugh away, dispelling gloom.

Bumblebees buzz, bringing news,
Of sunny days and playful views.
Together, we sip the morning dew,
Nature's love story, fresh and new.

Oh, the joy that simple plants bring,
Like a heartfelt song they sing.
In this garden where laughter thrives,
We craft sweet tales of our lives.

The Solace of Verdant Friendship

In my corner, she's rather stout,
With her green friend, there's no doubt.
We swap jokes as days go by,
In leafy whispers, we always sigh.

She says, "My spine's just part of the game!"
I chuckle, never calling her name.
We bask in our mossy humidity,
Is this friendship or just greenery?

When the rains come and puddles rise,
We splash like kids, oh what a surprise!
Her leaves glisten; it's quite the sight,
Nature's friends, a pure delight.

Together we thrive in pots so small,
Sharing laughs through every fall.
A duo made of chlorophyll cheer,
In this wild jungle, we shed a tear.

Love Grows in Unique Places

In the crack of the sidewalk, I found a friend,
With green little leaves that twist and bend.
She chuckles at the world so fast,
Resilient as weeds, she's built to last.

At brunch, we order sunshine and rain,
With a side of dirt for that earthy gain.
We toast to roots and blooms that won't stop,
Creating a dance on this flower shop.

As the sun dips low and the sky blushes pink,
Friendships flourish, what do you think?
In tiny spaces, joy takes its shape,
Oh love, in the oddest forms, we escape.

So here's to the quirks and spots we adore,
Finding laughter in nooks we explore.
With love that's wild and often misplaced,
In the garden of life, all's embraced.

Tapestry of Tender Greens

In a patchwork quilt of emerald delight,
Every leaf adds to the hilarity bright.
We snicker at thorns that prickle, yet play,
In this garden, we jest through the day.

Her pot is a podium where she stands tall,
Addressing all plants, both big and small.
With humor and wit, she blooms with glee,
Crafting tales of laughter, one leaf at a spree.

The ferns sway gently, they can't take a joke,
While the bumblebees buzz, both voracious and woke.
In this verdant realm where giggles collide,
We nurture good vibes that bloom far and wide.

So let's weave our joys in this leafy embrace,
Nature's jesters sharing the same space.
Finding bliss in the whispers and beams,
Together we create, in this tapestry of dreams.

Growth Amidst the Struggle

In the garden, I stumble and fall,
Tripping over pots, what a brawl!
Yet from the chaos, green shoots arise,
My plant life laughs at my clumsy tries.

With sun on my face and dirt on my knees,
I dance with the weeds, just doing as I please.
A sprout with a wink, a bloom with a grin,
In this funny jungle, I'll always win!

Soft Shadows of Affection

A little plant in the corner beams,
Casting hugs, or so it seems.
Every shadow twirls, with glee it prances,
Whispering secrets as my heart dances.

I stroke the leaves, a gentle tease,
It tickles my fingers, oh what a breeze!
In this leafy love fest, how sweet the game,
Who knew a houseplant could bring such fame?

Whispering Leaves

The leaves chatter softly, gossip in the sun,
About neighbors and critters, oh what fun!
I eavesdrop close, hear tales of delight,
As they wiggle and giggle, a leafy sight.

"Did you see that bee? Quite the flirt!"
Said one leaf high, in a way that won't hurt.
I chuckle and grin, they crack me up,
Nature's own sitcom, in a teacup.

Gentle Touch

A caress from a leaf feels like a dream,
Twirling around in a playful scheme.
Dancing in sunlight, a soft little tease,
Tickling my senses with such joyful ease.

The rough and smooth in this whimsical dance,
A prick here or there, but just take a chance!
With a chuckle, I giggle at life's silly bends,
For it's all in good fun, with the best of friends.

Thorns Guarding Sweetness

With a sigh and a grin, I approach the stash,
Knowing beneath thorns, there's treasure to clash.
They poke and they prod, oh what a ruckus,
Yet sweet is the fruit, so I'll risk the fuss.

In life's little garden, thorns play their part,
Guarding the sweetness, a tricky art.
I laugh at the pain, it's a funny ol' skit,
For every sharp joust, there's a treat to admit.

Nature's Affectionate Symphony

In the garden, plants do sway,
Whispering secrets in bright array.
Bees buzz like they've got jokes to tell,
While flowers giggle, oh so well.

The trees dance with floppy limbs,
Their leaves rustle like silly hymns.
Squirrels play tag, that's quite a sight,
While critters laugh till the fall of night.

Roses blush in a funny way,
Throwing petals like confetti play.
The sun grins down with a cheeky glow,
As nature's humor begins to flow.

So let's join in this wild parade,
We'll chuckle beneath the leafy shade.
Nature's heart is funny and bright,
In every bloom, pure delight!

Lush Love in the Sunlight

Under sunbeams, love takes flight,
Laughter echoes, oh what a sight!
Green vines tickle, they like to tease,
While daisies dance in the gentle breeze.

The butterflies flirt without a care,
Landing softly, like they're in a fair.
With every flutter there's a grin,
Nature's rituals, where fun begins!

Oh cacti poke with a playful sting,
While sunflowers waltz, they spin and swing.
Every leaf knows the art of jest,
In this garden, we are blessed!

So let's bask in this joy-filled space,
Laugh with the flowers, keep up the pace.
Beneath the sunlight, hearts take root,
In a playful symphony, oh how cute!

Resonance of Rooted Sentiments

Deep in the soil, roots intertwine,
Giggling softly, a love so divine.
Worms wiggle and sway in the muck,
Telling each other, 'This soil's just luck!'

Trees share tales of the winds they've known,
Barking out laughter, never alone.
Each shrub nods, feeling so spry,
In the echo of laughter, we all fly high.

The woodpecker pecks with a rhythmical beat,
Creating a tune, it's quite the treat.
Nature's orchestra, such a delight,
Playing sweet laughter into the night.

So come, gather round this leafy troupe,
Join the fun in this giggle-filled loop.
With every root, the joy will spread,
In the dance of life, we're gently led!

The Thicket of Tender Love

In the thicket where giggles bloom,
Bunny rabbits hop, making room.
Each one is a jester in fur so tight,
Playing hide and seek in the soft moonlight.

Thorns poke fun, yet love's still sweet,
While butterflies frolic on tiny feet.
Laughter echoes through leafy halls,
Nature's dance, where mischief calls.

Every vine whispers a cheeky joke,
As mistletoe winks—not just for folk!
Join the party, don't be shy,
This thicket's a blast, oh my oh my!

As shadows stretch and daylight fades,
The night fills with laughter in leafy glades.
With each rustling branch, the joy will stay,
In this thicket of love, we laugh and play!

Flourish Within

In the garden, weeds declare,
A party's brewing, Fred's not there.
We giggle as the snails collide,
A dance of chaos, joy and pride.

Petunias wearing silly hats,
Throwing shade at all the brats.
With bees that buzz a tune so sweet,
They dance like crazy on their feet!

Plump tomatoes plotting schemes,
To win the prize for biggest dreams.
While carrots laugh in rows so neat,
What fun it is to have a beet!

So let us grow and take our chance,
In this wild and wacky dance.
With roots that hug, we'll make a scene,
And chuckle at the garden green.

Essence of the Earth

Down by the creek, a frog sings loud,
Chasing flies, he's super proud.
A turtle grins from mossy rock,
While ants form lines to share their stock.

The flowers wear their brightest gowns,
Competing for the bee's crowns.
They trade their secrets, sweet and bold,
While laughing at the sun's warm gold.

A squirrel leaps, a boisterous show,
He thinks he's spry, but oh, oh no!
He misses branch and takes a drop,
With leaves that flutter, he won't stop!

So here's to nature's comical ways,
In every leaf, a laugh displays.
With joy that spreads across the land,
We find the fun, oh, isn't it grand?

Emotions in Bloom

One daisy dreamed of making pies,
Another offered witty lies.
Together stitched a laughter quilt,
With petals bright, the joy built.

A sunflower winks, its face so bright,
Claims it's the star of the moonlight.
The violets chuckle in their thrones,
While roses hum their haughty tones.

They play a game of leaf and vine,
Where every twist is oh-so-fine.
With humor draped like morning dew,
The garden thrives with mirth anew.

So let's embrace this joy so pure,
As blossoms laugh, we can't ignore.
In blooms of color, wit will soar,
With every joke, we want more!

Nature's Tender Touch

In the meadow where the grass tickles,
A lamb prancing, doing giggles.
Butterflies cha-cha in the sun,
While dandelions shoot for fun.

The brook babbles with clever puns,
As frogs join in with tiny runs.
The trees sway gently, teasing clouds,
While squirrels boast of acorn crowds.

Breezes whisper silly jokes,
Amidst the dance of playful folks.
With roots entwined, they share their winks,
As nature chuckles and life sinks.

In this wild and joyful place,
Where laughter leaves a soft embrace.
We'll revel in the earthy play,
With nature's touch, come what may!

Breathe in Serenity

In the garden of care, I skip with glee,
My pot of green wonders, oh so carefree.
A sip of calm, in the middle of noon,
Just me and my plants, dancing to the tune.

With leaves like smiles, they wave at me,
Whispering secrets, oh what a spree!
I water them gently, they drink like champs,
And laugh at my jokes, those little green tramps.

In this jungle of joys, I sprout my cheer,
A tender embrace, nothing to fear.
Here's to my pals, with their vibrant hues,
In the world of plants, I've nothing to lose.

So breathe in the peace, let laughter ignite,
With each little leaf, everything feels right.
In this quirky space, where silliness flows,
My happy sanctuary, where gratitude grows.

Green Velvet Reverie

In my plush little corner, sits a fine crew,
Each leaf a soft cushion, in shades green and blue.
They soak up my jokes like it's all they know,
With a twist and a turn, they steal the show.

They giggle in sunlight, a whimsical throng,
Creating a symphony, the weirdest of songs.
I shake up the room with my funniest quips,
While they nod in approval, with their leafy tips.

A vortex of whispers, they gossip and jest,
Turning my worries into a merry fest.
I'll sprinkle some water, we'll all have a blast,
In this plush little paradise, time moves too fast.

So here's to the plants, my green little squad,
With their velvet embrace, life feels like a façade.
In this bubbly cocoon, we play and we smile,
With my leafy companions, I'll stay for a while.

Whispers of Wellness

In the realm of green wonders, I giggle with glee,
Each plant a confidant, sharing life's decree.
They whisper in sunlight, tales of delight,
With every little leaf, my worries take flight.

A buddy with spiky hair, who loves to shake,
Telling me knock-knock jokes, for fun's sake.
I chuckle in rhythm, a silly duet,
With my leafy companions, no room for regret.

They sway with laughter, like humor divine,
In this joyful jungle, we utterly shine.
With pots full of punchlines, they cheer me on,
In this quirky little kingdom, worries are gone.

So let's toast to the greens, my giggly brigade,
In a world filled with laughter, we've got it made.
With whispers of wellness, and joy intertwined,
My heart's filled with laughter, forever aligned.

Soothing Shadows

In a nook of shadows, where giggles abound,
My leafy companions, oh what joy they've found.
They stretch in the sunlight, like kids in a park,
With each funny moment, they leave their mark.

They sway in the breeze, telling jokes with a twirl,
A green little gang, they give life a whirl.
While I tell them my secrets, they nod and agree,
These quirky green friends, my therapy spree.

With pots full of laughter, and smiles all around,
We dance in the kitchen, to their leafy sound.
Each leaf is a punchline, each stem a delight,
In this calamitous haven, everything's right.

So here's to the shadows, that cozy retreat,
Where humor and greenery make life so sweet.
In this fortress of friendship, we share our art,
With every little giggle, you'll soothe my heart.

The Garden of Quenching Souls

In the garden where laughter grows,
A plant with spines, but oh, it glows!
Water it well, it holds the key,
To sipping joy, just wait and see.

Feed it sunshine, give it cheer,
Watch it dance, have no fear!
Plant puns in soil, let joy sprout,
In this patch, let fun be about.

Thorns and Tenderness

A prickly friend, so bold and bright,
Hiding tears behind its plight.
With humor's touch and gentle tease,
It shares its charm with playful ease.

Soft as whispers, sharp as wit,
Bringing giggles, it won't quit!
Embrace the odd, the round and stout,
In thorns we find what life's about.

Beneath the Surface of Emotion

Underneath that spiky skin,
Lies a treasure, a silly grin.
Roots that tickle, stems that sway,
Let's dance around and laugh away.

Feelings bubbling, like a brew,
Serve them up with a wink or two.
A sip of joy, a giggle burst,
In this garden, laughter's thirst.

Resilience Wrapped in Greens

In leafy layers, strength does hide,
With jokes and jests, it takes the ride.
Bounce back bright, with every jest,
These green delights sure know the best.

Wrapped in humor, tough and sly,
A shield of greens that make you fly.
With every poke, a laugh unfolds,
In this tale of plant, be bold!

The Silent Language of Plants

In the garden, whispers bloom,
Leaves talk secrets, dispelling gloom.
Roots gossip under the ground,
Nature's chat where joy is found.

Sunlight winks, a playful tease,
Photosynthesis with the greatest ease.
Cacti crack jokes, dry and sharp,
While daisies dance, the floral harp.

Cultivated Connections

With clippings shared and pots exchanged,
Our friendship blossomed, unarranged.
In soil we trust, with compost laughs,
Tales of growth and tangled paths.

Pruned emotions, trimmed with care,
Watered dreams, we both can share.
A gardener's plot, a bond so bright,
Tending to roots, in morning light.

Harmony Between Spice and Softness

Basil and mint, a quirky pair,
One's a diva, the other rare.
Oregano rolls its eyes with sass,
While thyme just giggles as they pass.

Chili peppers bring the heat,
While lavender's calm, a gentle beat.
Together they stir a fragrant pot,
A spice rack party, laugh a lot!

Love in the Shadows of Green

In the jungle of leaves, a romance stirred,
A vine creeped close, not one word heard.
Ferns blush softly, in verdant delight,
Their flirtations blossom under moonlight.

The shy succulents share a glance,
In the cool shade, they start to dance.
A whisper of breezes, a rustle of leaves,
In the green twilight, love weaves.

Green Sanctuary

In my little garden, plants do cheer,
They dance and wiggle, never fear!
Forget the weeds, they're just a joke,
With every bloom, my heart they poke.

Cacti stand tall, like they've got style,
While succulents giggle, all the while.
They sip their water, oh so slow,
While I chase cats, to and fro!

The sun is shining, plants take a nap,
I slip on soil, and do a little clap.
With laughter ringing, the flowers sway,
In my green sanctuary, I'll stay!

The bugs are buzzing, creating tunes,
While carrots peek up, showing cartoons.
Each leaf is laughing, what a delight,
In this funny garden, all feels right.

Tender Succulent Whispers

Little green friends, they share their tales,
Of sun-soaked days and funny gales.
They whisper secrets, soft and sweet,
As I tiptoe by on clumsy feet.

They poke and prod, with spiky kin,
I laugh at how they're thick and thin.
A friendship formed with every touch,
Their gentle nudges mean so much.

They nod with joy when rain does come,
While I skip about, so full of fun.
Their tiny giggles fill the air,
As I try to dance without a care.

In every nook, a story's spun,
These tender whispers, oh what fun!
Their green embrace, a lovely sight,
In my succulent world, all feels right.

Embrace of the Earth

In the earth's embrace, I slip and slide,
With worms who wriggle, what a ride!
Each plant is winking, so full of glee,
As I tumble down with a comical plea.

The daisies shout, "Come join the fun!"
While dandelions laugh in the sun.
With roots intertwined, all snug as can be,
Nature's embrace, it's wild and free!

I wear a crown of leaves and cheer,
Though tangled twigs make things unclear.
In muddy puddles, I take a leap,
While happy buds my secrets keep.

The earth just giggles when I arrive,
With every harvest, I feel alive.
Nature's humor, a playful game,
In this lovely chaos, I find my fame!

Soothe the Soul

With every sprout, I hear a laugh,
As leaves play cards with their supportive staff.
They bask in sunshine, with roots in tune,
While I chase shadows beneath the moon.

The flowers gossip, sharing their flair,
While I stumble through without a care.
Their colors glow, lighting up the night,
A soothing balm, it feels so right.

The breeze carries chuckles, soft and clear,
As I talk to plants, wishing they'd hear.
They nod enthusiastically, with petals wide,
In this funny patch, love can't hide!

Here in the garden, wild and bold,
I find my laughter, as stories unfold.
With every bloom, the joy takes flight,
Soothe the soul with plant-filled delight!

Renewal of the Spirit

A plant in the sun, what a sight,
With leaves so bright, a pure delight.
It stretches and yawns, wakes from its nap,
Spreading joy like a playful clap.

In the kitchen it sits, a loyal guard,
Makes me chuckle, it's not that hard.
It whispers, "Do more, stop being a couch!"
I can't help but grin, like a happy slouch.

Water me, feed me, it begs with a wink,
While I munch on chips and a soda drink.
Yet every time I glance at its hue,
It cracks me up, with its greenish view.

A silly plant with the spirit so spry,
Teaching me how not to be shy.
Renewal in laughter, that's its art,
With a smile so wide, it opens my heart.

Soft Green Emotions

In the garden, green giggles abound,
Waving softly without a sound.
They dance in the breeze, cheeky and spry,
Whispering secrets as they sway by.

Each leaf a smile, broad and wide,
With silly antics they cannot hide.
They tease and they tickle, gentler than air,
Bringing joy and laughter, beyond compare.

When I get moody, they sway just right,
Wrapping me up in their leafy light.
"Oh come on, lighten up!" they sing and shout,
Turning my frown upside down, no doubt.

Soft emotions, oh how they jive,
In my green friends, I feel alive.
With each little quirk, they play their part,
Filling my days with a funny heart.

Gentle Thorns of Affection

In every hug, a secret sting,
With gentle thorns, they do their thing.
Love wrapped up in a spiky embrace,
Laughter emerges in this quirky space.

A prick here and there, oh what a tease,
Yet wrapped in humor, it's all a breeze.
Affection blooms in the oddest of ways,
With a chuckle, they brighten my days.

Don't be alarmed by a little poke,
These thorns are wrapped in a funny joke.
It's love in disguise, simply absurd,
A punchline waiting to be heard.

With each gentle prod, my worries fade,
In the garden of joy, my fears are laid.
So here's to the thorns, the laughter they bring,
In the heart of the plant, there's always some zing!

Serenity Blooms in Silence

In quiet corners, soft laughter grows,
With silent blooms in endless rows.
There's peace nestled under leafy crowns,
A comical pause in the hustle of towns.

They wiggle and giggle, just out of sight,
With a hint of mischief, pure delight.
When the world gets noisy, they take a pause,
In their tranquil silence, they find applause.

Sipping sunshine in their green attire,
With nature's humor, they never tire.
They chuckle softly, no need to shout,
In the calm of the garden, they dance about.

Serenity blooms with a wink and grin,
In this oasis, my joy begins.
Among the quiet, under the tree,
Life's funny little secrets are shared with glee.

Garden of Solace

In the garden, I trip and fall,
Amidst the weeds, I hear them call.
"Hey there, friend! Don't take it hard,
Just brush off leaves - it's not a yard!"

With every bloom, a chuckle grows,
The blooms all giggle, who really knows?
They poke and prod, all in good jest,
In their silly dance, I feel so blessed.

Silken Green Embrace

In a world so soft, my worries fade,
Wrapped in green, like a leafy braid.
The plants all whisper, "Don't you fret,
Life's a joke – a funny set!"

Branches sway with a gentle grin,
Tickling my cheek, pulling me in.
They tease and twirl, a leafy spree,
In their embrace, I'm wild and free.

The Heart's Oasis

In the sunlit patch where giggles sprout,
The cacti dance, there's no doubt.
"Prickly friends, they call us stout!
But we bring cheer, come join the clout!"

In this oasis, laughter breeds,
With everyone's quirks, there are no weeds.
We sip on joy, a funny brew,
Sharing secrets, just me and you.

Calm in the Chaos

Amidst the tumble, I find my peace,
The leaves wave hello, a warm release.
"Does chaos fright? Just laugh and soar!
Join our quirk parade - there's always more!"

Beneath the flutter, light as a feather,
Find solace in jokes, we're all together.
In this mad world, share the delight,
In the funny dance, everything's right.

The Rooted Embrace of Devotion

In a pot by the door, there lives a plant,
With leaves that can dance and a quirky slant.
It tickles my toes when I walk by,
Whispering secrets, oh my, oh my!

Its spikes could deter, but it's soft at the core,
Like a friend who's a bit of a bore.
We laugh at the sun, we bask in its glow,
With a twist of a stem, we put on a show!

Growing together, we share all our snacks,
I swear it can hear all my silly quacks.
A loyal companion, it doesn't complain,
Just drinks from my mishaps like rain on a drain.

Though rooted in soil, in silliness thrive,
My leafy buddy makes me feel alive.
Through laughter and joy, our bond has grown tight,
A truly strange pairing, but oh, what a sight!

Sweet Sustenance from Nature's Heart

With a sprinkle of care, I nurture you right,
You help me survive through each laugh and fright.
Your green little fingers, they reach for the sky,
While I feed you jokes that make crickets cry!

In the morning light, we share a big grin,
I promise each leaf that it's destined to win.
Your sassy demeanor, your plump little face,
We giggle together in our sunny space.

I pour you some water, but sometimes I splash,
You know my antics—it's quite the comedic clash.
Through ups and downs, in silliness bonded,
With each little sprout, our friendship's not fronded.

You bring me such joy, like a sweet cupcake,
Oh, the recipe's wild, it's a delightful flake.
In your green life, I find laughter and cheer,
My lovely green pal, forever sincere!

In Bloom with Shared Affection

We're blooming together, my friend and I,
You laugh at my puns, you really can't lie.
With petals a-swaying, and roots intertwined,
In each playful breeze, our joys are aligned.

A burst of green laughter where mischief is brewed,
We share funny stories of life's little food.
With every new sprout, a giggle we find,
You're the happiest plant that I've ever designed!

In the garden of wits, we frolic and play,
While the sun shines down on our bright cabaret.
Prickly yet lovely, your charm shines so bright,
Together we shine, in our own comical light.

So here's to the blooms, to laughter and cheer,
My lovely green buddy, I'm glad that you're near.
In this quirky garden, we'll always make art,
As roots of affection weave deep in my heart!

Oasis of Emotional Growth

In the dry desert air, we thrive side by side,
With laughs and some water, our spirits collide.
You stretch out your limbs, a sparkly display,
As I tell you the tales from my funny old days.

Our oasis of joy, where mirth is the fuel,
Brush off the dust, we're no longer a duel.
With roots in the soil, and smiles on our face,
We blend kinda crazy in this sun-kissed place.

Each leaf brings a chuckle, a hearty delight,
Together we blossom, oh what a sight!
With humor as compost, we'll flourish and grow,
In this wacky little patch, we put on a show.

So let's giggle and dance with the breeze on our backs,
In this haven of laughter, we'll never relax.
With each tender moment, a smile from the heart,
In the garden of friendship, we'll never part!

www.ingramcontent.com/pod-product-compliance
Lightning Source LLC
Chambersburg PA
CBHW070311120526
44590CB00017B/2629